salmonpoetry

Diverse Voices from Ireland and the World

Corvus and Crater

ERIN COUGHLIN HOLLOWELL

Published in 2023 by
Salmon Poetry
Cliffs of Moher, County Clare, Ireland
Website: www.salmonpoetry.com
Email: info@salmonpoetry.com

ISBN 978-1-915022-31-8

Cover Image: *Keeper of the Key* by Sally Banfill – https://banfill.com/
Cover Design & Typesetting: *Siobhán Hutson Jeanotte*

Printed in Ireland by Sprint Print

to voices missed and missing

Acknowledgements

"A dissolving language," "Erasing the words as she writes them," and "We once believed in binomials" were originally published in some form in *Barren Magazine*. "When she pages backward," "Solitary its completion," and "Prime is not just the number" were originally published in *EcoTheo Review*. "Choir hive" was originally published in *Orion Magazine*. "Instructions for compass truing" was originally published in *Split Rock Review*. "Ritual for accounting for the plumb-line," "Ritual for washing hands with starlight," and "Ritual to shackle the greater bear" were originally published in some form in *The Stony Thursday Poetry Book* No. 18. "Corvus and crater" "The way we recognize each other," and "History of defiance" were originally published in *Terrain.org*.

I'd like to thank the Rasmuson Foundation which continues to support individual artists and writers in Alaska, as well as all of the amazing women of Storyknife whose passion for the written word sustains me. I am grateful to Elizabeth Bradfield, Lauren Camp, and Andrew Wyeth for their incisive comments on this collection. A thousand and one thank yous to Peggy Shumaker who has been a true friend throughout my writing career. Thank you to Sherry Simpson who could always talk me off the ledge; dear friend, without you I must find my own wings. Much gratitude to Jessie Lendennie and Siobhán Hutson Jeanotte for your hard work at Salmon Poetry that has created such a rich and beautiful home for poetry in Ireland and abroad – go raibh maith agaibh. And finally, thank you to Glenn who supports my writing, is patient when I am a caged beast because I am not writing, and who supplies me with endless room to devote to my craft.

Contents

1

Corvus and crater

Roadside prophet, hag-stones and feathers
rattle you
        along. Until evening
you find your tree, birch, spruce, or alder
and thereon perch. Or curl
                into wild
rose or raspberry thicket.
              Tell us,
who loves the keyhole over the key?

Ritual for the measuring expansion

Let us talk. Let us tie it all up
so that even the sharpest
                         sword can
not sunder. Or better, let us sit
in silence and watch
                         these stars spinning
their own telling. We can listen, ears
open to what endures,
                         what becomes.

Prime is not just the number

Ocean water branches in bloodstream.
A tree climbs
           from a cave. Such struggle
in the absence of absence. Too full
she is now, solid and smoke.
                        Beget
the begetter, back to beginning.
That older testament split open.

Navigation of certain bold species

Wonder wander and she goes
                              along
the path, scent carried inside helix,
later unspooled
                    beneath a low sky.
Let them say magnetic.
                        Say pulling.
She only understands her cell spells:
a tang like brass moonlight on reaped fields.

Ritual for accounting for the plumb-line

Map wing path, sky's hachures and circuit.
Find where your trail overlaps with Crow's
concentric circles
                     of pain-weaving.
Is it bloodwork or blind reckoning?
Nettle, yarrow, and devil's
                           club know.
The broken hare under the elder.

Future provisioning

Unobstructed vault. She tries to find
the line between blush
                    and blue, one more
impossible morning task. Bolting
her armor back together. Saying
she never wanted
                    to sing with them.
Forgotten churches built of updraft.

Hours after her name is called

She thinks of this as a gift. Open
any cabinet and a wren
                              might
fly out. Not like a loaded gun. More
like a dream of her mother sitting
in a darkened
                        room with her eyes shut
against withering. Which comes. Which comes

Designed for initiation

Crow dreams of her own bright book,
                                  scripture
of flotsam reeling in surf, of wind
rattling the spruce. A song tickling god's
ear, her skritch
                     skritch over the compost's
breath in the freezing air. Her only
commandment:
                seek opportunity.

The rotten handle on the scythe

Where did the snake go in the winter
when apples shriveled
                    beneath the snow?
The garden even more silent, lost
in remembering
                    the way she hummed
as she made her
                    way to the river.
Who tells that story of winding now?

2

She bleak breaks

In a stand of nine spruce, at least four
over-burdened with cones. The siskins
ornament such
     trees with flickering
and their shattered smattering
       of song.
Wind from back of the bay
       arrows steel,
beats the bleached grass and weeds in ditches.

In a flat cap and suspenders with his arms crossed

Memory gate.
        Stone stained with iron
tears.
    Stone upon which she finds music
grimed with a desperate roadway. The miles
fold in on each other, tucked among
strata cut
      by her great grandfather's
hands while he sang deafened and dirty.

Sainthood made of isobars

After she finds
        her edges, the smudge
of moon-glint through spindrift remembers
herself to herself. Like a blunt print
of a careless god's thumb. She
                  never
meant to let go of her miracle.
Wings made of darkness stitched to her back.

Innermost architecture

Most like a prow, her house leaned against
the storm, wind buffet and timber creak.
A face abstract and withheld,
                              even
the woodstove sullen. She tucked each fold
of herself in. Blasts slammed
                              into spruce.
She could feel
                the roots of her life shift.

Charts curled up at the edges

Full moon rising through Eridanus.
Fool boy long
              smoldered into story.
Who names the stars? Pins legends to them?
Her mouth
              puddles with incarnation,
wren flicker through alderwood leaf drift,
spider winds
              ruin's bright rehearsal.

A box of snapped matches and one burnt nub

Guttering.
        Thumping every black key
on the ghost piano. She might drown
in the pool she's conjured. Little flame
that only yearned to burn down
                       the whole
world. Now she can merely push around
the shadows. Make them dance.
                Let them die.

A dissolving language

Before sunrise, anything could be
Crow. Eldritch creep of hoar-frost along
slate seams and still
                     the light is swallowed.
Dim chills the pulsebeat. Rosehips shrunken
and unpalatable.
                 Crow wonders
down dream pathways, not this door
                         nor that.

The unpredictable solicitude
of decomposition

Sometimes the weather just wipes
                          away
the road. Or maybe she lost the map.
Either way, there is one
                          shadow so
great, she lives inside it and calls it
home. It chips away
                          at the edges,
but she keeps moving her feet and hands.

Ritual to fracture the prescribed lexicon

Smooth between finger, silver to see,
branches tumbled and spumed,
                            wracked above
tide-line and knotted amidst ghost gear.
Pull one loose like an ogham stave, then peer
at this fate
              tossed up from the blind sea.
Wood-bound she is, once rooted, now loft.

3

In columns like a ledger

Is it enough to reach? Disaster
conveyed
       by our tempest. What was once
solid suddenly a precipice.
We say grounded to imply
            a type
of steadiness. When a tree falls,
               roots
rend surface, reveal what earth anchored.

Relic neighborhood

Unsurprised by
              its weight, but colder
and older than she'd imagined. No
answer needed. The fire long gone out.
She dug a small hold
                for to serve as
a small house. Scaffold with bones. Windows
of ice. Want lives strong
                   in the waiting.

Beneath the skin dwells a feral energy

Snow-thicket cathedral at midnight.
What alters
            the imagination
alters everything. What is contained
in the hare's prayer,
                now white in winter,
that did not exist in brown autumn?
Owl wing salvation,
                rustle breath swerve.

Ritual for washing hands with starlight

The mountainside leaned
                    against the light
like a dun cow. Everywhere she went
there were empty saucers tucked into
hedges or around corners.
                            Branches
wound with torn ribbons. She might find crow
feathers in her sleeve
                    when the sun rose.

Advice from a rusted pail and candy-wrapper

What if a wish kept calling her back?
Dropping her car keys.
                      Slipping on ice
in the post office parking lot. Bell
of coffee before
                   sunrise. She wants
each minute to live in her. How you
stand here is important.
                   So stand here.

Holding a line taut

Wren leaves three strokes of calligraphy
in fresh snow. A small velocity.
An essay on brevity.
                      Sunrise
so late that morning is one long,
                                low
wound. Glaze clenches on alder branches.
You are listening from beyond death.

Erasing the words as she writes them

Each mountain trails
                    a veil of spindrift
tethered to high cold wind. It could be
that there is only one word they speak,
but who could climb high enough and
                                        still
be humble enough to listen. Crow
heard the word, and maybe,
                        understood.

Ritual for summoning the winter circle

Threshold journey. If those stars be cold,
then question warmth. Consider
                              what breeds
from gust and slash. Kneel there in the bow,
fix focus
                on rumble of cobbles
fondled by tide-wash. You may find this
unmapping. Wrack snagged
                        among blowdown.

She read it in their eyes

Each tree a river of sun hidden.
As a child, she burrowed into duff
and dreamt branches.
                        Or climbed up until
rocking, she breathed. To be gravity-
shackled, to be rootless and
                              inert,
is poison-sore, galled, rotten within.

4

Ritual for lost landscape

Stolen rowan, plucked for its red gift
in the grey static of this icescape
to create
       a door transplanted.
                  Speak
shovel that breaks the iron soil.
                  Speak
inhospitable hole. What comes forth?
Woman that carries both weal and woe.

There is the body and the unbodied

Ten below zero, dawning becomes
a bell silenced. Even her breath hangs
for just a moment,
                then is dampened.
She knows the current is there, hidden,
and all around her are brief
                      lives. Night
empties her, death's gracious final
shrug.

A vessel without a name

Tell her where the myth
                        has fled and Crow
will remember. Petal-wet inside
the thigh, wide-eyed with imagining.
Crow sits watching on the very
                                        tip
of a spruce tree.
                        What is her portion?
Song, string, stirring
                        of midwinter snow.

Maybe the shadows are evidence

Things grow
            in gaps.
                        Gullies where water
sings the fractured-crystal branching of
lichen all through winter. Solstice sun
draws up between two
                            mountains, reflects
snow to sea, sea to snow,
                            then shift stall.
Shallow arc to plunge back to the dark.

Companion to Castor

If she woke as golden-crowned kinglet
inside the deep spruce locked with hoarfrost,
would she see doubt?
     Would the night be full
of the clank and drag of her thoughts, then?
Rather, would she tend her tiny flame,
little arsonist of ice season.

Ritual for setting up the wheeling

A birthday celebration, they say.
Details handed down in story,
                  songs,
and yet a million times death dealt here
by unkindness.
              Snow gathering deep.
We call it white and praise it.
                    A stone
has a hymn too, ringing deep below.

A hand pushing firmly against a chest

Let new year come with its silvern storms
smoothing snow curve-wise curled. Drifts along
garden fences. Swales where the road frays.
Let each person
                    attend to their own
blank page.
                Watch as footsteps are erased.
Siskins let weather inform their flight.

Solitary its completion

Behind her house, about five yards up
a steep hill, a birch tree listens
                        all
day and through the frozen night. The stars
tap upon it like cold silver spoons.
Beith, beginning,
                  unlonely in its
vigil. Companion to remaining.

Calendar sangboc

Crow lifts her wing to pull up the sun
from its warm bed. Minus
                              three degrees
and the new year crackling. Forget
                                        dates.
Forget
        years. Throw clocks in the dust bin.
Come forth
                all you ragged things to dance.
Rise up, barefoot, quickened in streamlight.

5

Stories beneath the stories

Ice stuttering. Inside the ragged
forest, the wolf's foot.
                          Her hunger is
prisms, needles, dendrites, stellar plates.
Every numb heart crouches still, waiting
for shatter. It will be
                          warmer there,
in the wolf's mouth, kiss of blood's summer.

History of defiance

Crow comes from the place where light dimples.
Mountaintops winked
                          away in snow's silk
dangled by clouds, dragged across summit
until much is simply
                          effaced. Then
from what swirled squalls have disappeared, Crow
comes clapping
                          her black wings like laughter.

Most like an erratic

The river is snow sluice,
                          silt silken
among the stones on which she washes.
The blood
            was never vaunted, symbol
of no quickening, no sacrifice.
The sky, a flat pan of beaten tin
and still she scrubs,
                          voice casting split snare.

Ritual for grinding wheat into flour

Hushed is the bluest hour as minutes
sift crystal-drift. Patterns.
                                Arc and sweep,
alders along the muted creekside.
Empty cup. Broken mirror.
                                Member.
Remember. The tide of breath. Inhale.
Anything
                is possible. Exhale.

Complex correspondences hereby simplified

Our sleeves unraveling, ridden hard
by winter's toothed wind, we fetch
                              against
any spot of sun or glowing patch
before the hearthstone.
                    Let's imagine
honey, elder blossoms, a mad whirl
of gnats above summer's fat garden.

Choir hive

Against white sky, the birch tree opens
its many dark

        mouths. She hears its words,
golden river under snow. Secret
honey. Clapper of vein-scribed marble,
that bell rings

        each full moon.

                Now waning.
Now feeding the mountain underneath.

We once believed in binomials

Crow picks up a stick and heads for sand
to scratch out the math.
                        One: we are meat.
Two: time moves in a straight line outward.
Solve for:
          we are all going to die.
And too soon.
                 Corollary: the sun
chases after the moon's
                    pocket change.

A hum below the level of hearing

March. Frigid sun sullens from one bruise
to another. As if
                    performing
that rare kind of light that unhinges.
Taxicab light on long
                        empty fares.
We twist
          and twist to find some handhold.
One apple. A handful of almonds.

The elegant lace of persistence

She had never learned to build a fire
in the wood stove. Squat lengths of split
                                   spruce
glower and refuse to catch. From out
the firebox, a moth flutters
                        just as
she puts match to paper twist. The flames
swift up to catch it,
                  cinder on wings.

6

Call her the littlest hunter-gatherer

When she turns the corner,
                         the corner
turns her. Leaf-raddled, duff underfoot,
one eye blinks and disappears. An owl
was spelling earlier,
                         now a thrush
stitches himself into the ear. Who
listens on this side of the river?

Famous partners for dance lessons

The tug when a root lets go, an ease
pulling free
                into bright air, a hole
left behind. Celebrate the wise
                                soil
cupping its new emptiness dreaming.
Light penetrating.
                Dark receiving.
No saint, no sinner, to be rendered.

Ritual for the last bridge home

You become a deer,
                  a salmon, take
flight from a flat gray lake,
                      wings rushing
to meet yourself anew. What mirror
could keep up with the changes wrought by
your god.
          All the ways your myth demands
another sacrifice. One more life.

The way we recognize each other

Time owns
         a vast labyrinth, scented
with beeswax and rain on rotted wood
planks. Crow likes to dance there.
                  She's humming
some rough song. One-two-three.
                  One-two-three.
Memory.   Memory.   Memory.
Then the whomp of her wings as she leaves.

Know how to count the measure

Is she the mask or the swept feather?
Music sweeps through.
                      Tiny destruction
follows her home. Out of season thrush
that breaks itself
                    against her window.
Singing can bring shatter, too.
                         A gap
through which a thousand soft things could fly.

What she carries in her suitcase

She learns to face the light.
                                  Horizon
flicker or brazen bolt. Though she was
taught that all is smudge, is filth, a kind
of tale devoid of stars,
                                        she studies
bean seedlings. Studies sparrows. Dawn comes.
Night follows.
                          Trusts earth to heedless spin.

Perhaps an expression of the common self

As the voices rise out
            of the hole,
mist echo mulch distress leak brilliant,
she tilts her left ear to heed,
                wanting
to parse memory and forgetting.
We break the world
            again. She's hearing
dream language, tidewater
                balancing.

When she pages backward

Mostly scattered. Smear. The death of one
thing is the beginning of something
else.
      Nettle lush in storm-water ditch.
Misplaced knife of memory.
               Alder
cones pulled apart by bird beaks.
               Morning,
arbitrary, porous boundary.

Ritual to shackle the greater bear

Let us take four branches from alders
to build a house. Let us
                    take four stones
from the creek bed to court us music,
founder it on mud slick, bind it with
a silver coin
              at each sunk corner.
Offer these bodies to solid earth.

ERIN COUGHLIN HOLLOWELL is a poet and writer who lives at the end of the road in Alaska. Prior to landing in Alaska, she lived on both US coasts, in big cities and small towns, pursuing many different professions from tapestry weaving to arts administration. She is the author of two earlier collections, *Pause, Traveler* (2013) and *Every Atom* (2018), both published by Boreal Books. Her work has been most recently published in *Stony Thursday, Poetry Ireland Review, Orion Magazine, Prairie Schooner, EcoTheo Review, Alaska Quarterly Review, Terrain.org,* and the Academy of American Poets Poem-A-Day website. In 2013 and 2018, Hollowell was awarded a Rasmuson Foundation Fellowship by the Rasmuson Foundation and in 2013, a Connie Boochever Award by the Alaska State Council on the Arts. She was one of the inaugural recipients of the Alaska Literary Awards in 2014. Currently, she is a Black Earth Institute fellow. She is the executive director of Storyknife Writers Retreat and director of the Kachemak Bay Writers' Conference.

salmonpoetry

Cliffs of Moher, County Clare, Ireland

"Publishing the finest Irish and international literature."
Michael D. Higgins, President of Ireland